September

Months of the Year

by Mari Kesselring
Illustrated by Ronnie Rooney

Content Consultant:
Susan Kesselring, MA
Literacy Educator and Preschool Director

magic wagon

visit us at www.abdopublishing.com

Published by Magic Wagon, a division of the ABDO Group, 8000 West 78th Street, Edina, Minnesota 55439. Copyright © 2010 by Abdo Consulting Group, Inc. International copyrights reserved in all countries. All rights reserved. No part of this book may be reproduced in any form without written permission from the publisher.

Looking Glass Library™ is a trademark and logo of Magic Wagon.

Printed in the United States.

 PRINTED ON RECYCLED PAPER

Text by Mari Kesselring
Illustrations by Ronnie Rooney
Edited by Holly Saari
Interior layout and design by Emily Love
Cover design by Emily Love

Library of Congress Cataloging-in-Publication Data

Kesselring, Mari.
  September / by Mari Kesselring ; illustrated by Ronnie Rooney ; content consultant, Susan Kesselring.
    p. cm. — (Months of the year)
  ISBN 978-1-60270-636-1
  1. September—Juvenile literature. 2. Calendar—Juvenile literature. I. Rooney, Ronnie, ill. II. Kesselring, Susan. III. Title.
  CE13.K49 2010
  398'.33—dc22

                          2008050697

Do you know the
12 months of the year?
Are you ready to learn?
Then keep reading here!

Do you know what month
is number nine?
Try to guess it.
You will do just fine!

Did you say September?

Wow! You are smart.

Do you want to learn about this month?

Let's start!

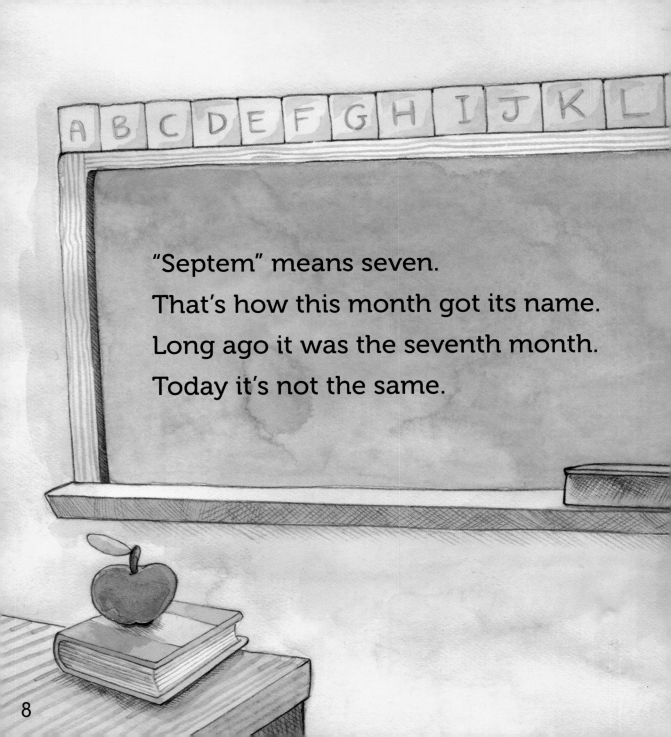

"Septem" means seven.
That's how this month got its name.
Long ago it was the seventh month.
Today it's not the same.

Labor Day is September's first Monday.

It has a perk.

On this day, some people
do not have to work.

September is when many kids go back to school. It is also when the weather starts to turn cool.

Listen to the leaves
crunch under your feet.
The first day of fall is in September.
How neat!

One day in September is Grandparents Day.
Send them a letter if they live far away.

Some people enjoy
holidays in September.
Rosh Hashanah is a
good one to remember.

Hispanic Heritage Month
is this time of year.
We have a fiesta
and give a big cheer!

The 30th day means
September is done.
But don't get too sad.
There's still lots of fun!

Back to School

Are you ready to go back to school? Are you excited to meet your new teacher? Draw a picture or make a card for him or her. It will help you get to know each other. It is a great way to start the school year!

Fiesta!

Having a fiesta is a great way to learn about Hispanic heritage. Ask your parents to help you throw a fiesta for you and your friends.

Words to Know

fiesta—a Spanish word that means "party."
heritage—the handing down of something from one generation to the next.
perk—an added benefit.
Rosh Hashanah—the Jewish New Year.

Web Sites

To learn more about September, visit ABDO Group online at **www.abdopublishing.com**. Web sites about September are featured on our Book Links page. These links are routinely monitored and updated to provide the most current information available.